Praise for *When t|*

If all Christian non-fi‹
fill the bestseller lists
transparent. Life-changing story.

—Kerry McKibbon
Pastor's Wife, Evangel Pentecostal Church
Brantford, Ontario

This book is a must-read for any person who has had their life turned upside-down because of a loved one's addiction. As a mother of a daughter with an addiction, Judy bravely outlines this journey and also captures the central role her faith played during this time.

—Lindsay Serbu
Family Intervention Specialist
Concurrent Disorders Outreach Team Supervisor
St. Leonard's Community Services
Addiction and Mental Health Programs

In God's creative plan, He chose that you would be a mother. He puts that child in your arms and it costs you everything. You pour your life into that child and you have big dreams and plans. God has made us so that we would do anything for our child, and through the years we experience joy, as well as pain. Then, as every child is destined to individualize, they gradually become responsible for their own lives. They, like you, will stand alone before God and make their choices. They will go through experiences, but God will never leave them. He loves them more than you do. He has an individual plan, not only for this life but for eternity.

—Rev. Lorne Shepherd
Author and Founder of Heart to Heart Family Ministries

WHEN THE LIGHT
at the end of
THE TUNNEL
is another *train*

*A Mother's Faith Journey Through
her Daughter's Addiction*

JUDY TOMCZAK

WHEN THE LIGHT AT THE END OF THE TUNNEL IS ANOTHER TRAIN
Copyright © 2015 by Judy Tomczak

Names of family members have been changed to respect privacy.

ISBN: 978-1-4866-0782-2

Word Alive Press
131 Cordite Road, Winnipeg, MB R3W 1S1
www.wordalivepress.ca

WORD ALIVE
—P R E S S—

Library and Archives Canada Cataloguing in Publication

Tomczak, Judy, 1962-, author
    When the light at the end of the tunnel is another train : a mother's faith journey through her daughter's addiction / Judy Tomczak.

Issued in print and electronic formats.
ISBN 978-1-4866-0782-2 (pbk.).--ISBN 978-1-4866-0783-9 (pdf).--ISBN 978-1-4866-0784-6 (html).--ISBN 978-1-4866-0785-3 (epub)

    1. Drug abuse. 2. Substance abuse. 3. Parenting--Religious aspects--Christianity. 4. Mothers and daughters. I. Title.

HV5824.Y68T65 2015   362.29   C2014-908406-4
                                                C2014-908407-2

While this book is based on a true story, my story, and my perspective, I have not used my daughter's real name and have left out other names to protect the privacy of those in my story.

CONTENTS

DEDICATION

I dedicate this book to my husband, Ron, who stepped into our mess and never looked back. His words over and over to me were "I'm not going anywhere." He loves my girls as though they were his own and has journeyed with me through their turbulent teenage years, and into their adult years. Ron has been a source of strength to me. He is my hero, never making a situation worse, always providing support, a warm hug, wise words, and a chuckle in times of turmoil.

To my daughters, whom I cannot imagine my life without. They both have unique awesomeness and struggles that make them so very special to me, and they are each on their own individual journey. Even though the journey has been excruciatingly difficult at times, I would do it all over again. I love them no matter what, as they are mine and I consider them both a gift. A mother's love knows no bounds, though love sometimes doesn't feel warm and fuzzy.

I thank God for my parents, who brought me up in a Christian home. Without my faith, I don't know how I would have made it through. I thank my two best friends, Andrea and Gabrielle, who God brought into my life in my teens, and we are together still. My prayer chain, my shoulders of support, without judgement, without ceasing… they have always been there.

What would life be like without my brother and sister, who through the years kept me humble with their brotherly and sisterly teasing? They have always been in my corner. Without exception, when we get together, we laugh until our sides hurt.

Thank you, Sam, for your encouragement to share my story. You are a light in my life and a constant encouragement. You are special. Thank you, Kerry, my new friend, close to home and close to my heart. Thank you, Joanne, for sharing your story, which made me feel for the first time like I wasn't alone.

This book was my therapy, and I want to share it with the countless mothers and grandmothers who share a similar story to mine. I have met you in unexpected places and I'm always inspired by our common bond. We come from all walks—broken families, intact families, wealthy, and in need—but we are all the same. We love our children, and so often the light at the end of the tunnel is another train. We have struggled to save them, and have been wounded in battle, yet we go on to fight another day because as long as there is breath, there is hope.

INTRODUCTION

Writing is my therapy. Through the years of this battle with my daughter and her addictions, and all the chaos that it brought home, I have written much. Some of it I have shared with people who were in similar situations. I'm a survivor of adultery, divorce, and parenting alone, all of which were heart-breaking—but nothing beat me up more than my daughter's battle with addiction.

I've learned so much throughout this journey about God's unconditional love for us and His strength. I've learned that just when I think I cannot go on another day, because the pain in my heart is just too much, He gives me what I need to keep going.

This book is not a beginning-to-end type of book, but rather a compilation of what I've written on the journey. It is my gift to you, in hopes that it will encourage you to hang in there and fight the fight. With God's help, you will get through it. It will often feel like the light at the end of the tunnel is just another train, more painful at times than you think you can bear, but with God's help and your trust in Him, you will survive.

As you read, I hope you feel a connection and know that you are not alone. I hope you are inspired.

BEFORE I BEGIN

I cannot begin this journey without sharing how much I love her. Ashley is my firstborn and I wouldn't trade her for anything. I once had a nightmare towards the end of my pregnancy with her. I woke from a very real and tormenting dream in which someone was trying to kill my unborn child. It's the kind of dream you don't forget because it was so horrific. It left me with a feeling about her that I couldn't shake… a worry, a concern for her life, though I didn't really know why I had it.

Before I share with you all the things that are ugly and hurtful and destructive, here is how I see her. When you think of her, see what I see.

While it is true that I've had many struggles with Ashley, there is another side. There's what I see when I look at her, and what I know to be true about her. There is her soul, and a life I know will someday bear fruit. This is what I see as her mother, and what I believe her creator also sees.

When you think of her, see what I see. I see a little girl who at a young age was wounded deeply by those she trusted most. I see a little girl who didn't know how to deal with the pain inside her and acted out in the only way she knew how.

I remember a little girl who had, and still has, a very giving heart. She's the same little girl who prayed faithfully every day for an aunt whom everyone else had given up on. I remember a little girl who cared to notice that her student teacher didn't have decent shoes to wear and at Christmas time insisted we give her a pair of mine.

I remember a troubled teen who gave her heart to those who used her and abused her, yet when those same people ended up in jail she's the one who went to visit them and comfort them.

She is gifted with a beautiful voice and sings like an angel. She is beautiful and funny and smart and full of potential. She is an awesome mother.

She was a child filled with talent. She took to dance, figure skating, track and field, cross-country running, and horseback riding as though her life depended on it. She even taught herself to play the piano by ear. She was a little girl who could have done anything but ended up doing none of it because deep down there was a little child who believed she didn't deserve it.

I am her mother, and I love her dearly. I see her suffering, I see her mistakes, I feel her hurt, and I love her still. No one can judge her but God Himself, as none of us have ever walked a day in her shoes. Every one of us has walked a different journey. None of us can ever know for sure if we would or wouldn't have made the same choices as another, had our journey been the same.

She gave her heart to the Lord as a little girl, and therefore I believe she belongs to Him. Just as I have fought so many battles to save her, cried so many tears, my God fights for her harder and never rests. Even if she was the only one out there lost, He would fight for her still. He never says, "I've had enough." He never says, "I can't do this anymore."

chapter one

A QUIET MOMENT

I HARDLY KNOW WHAT TO DO WITH MYSELF. THE HOUSE IS STILL, everyone is safe and doing their own thing. My world, you might say, is still and yet I'm not quite sure how to deal with that and how to be still myself. A crisis... now there's something I've become comfortable and familiar with.

I've learned to rest with one eye open. A skill learned as a young teenager while being camp counsellor to a group of teenage girls. I'd sleep at night with one eye open so I could keep an eye on those who tried to sneak out of the cabin to meet boys while they thought I was sound asleep. They were always amazed they couldn't get past me.

I can't remember when I started using the skill as an adult. It's like looking over my shoulder waiting for the next ball to drop. Never quite able to enjoy the good times because I know something is looming around the next corner. After a while, you begin to expect it.

I never had this skill as a child, because I never needed it. Life was predictable, safe, and secure. We were a typical Christian family—a father, mother, sister, and brother. We were, of course, forced against our will to go to church every Sunday morning and Sunday night, and usually some time midweek for children's programs—and later on, the greatly anticipated youth group activities, which we actually did enjoy.

I remember vividly being so angry with my parents, mostly my father, for dragging me to church on Sunday nights, because I never got to watch *The Wonderful World of Disney* like the rest of my friends at school. My brother thought my father was very uncool, because he didn't get drunk and swear like the rest of his friends' dads. Can you imagine thinking that?

Now my heart is filled with gratefulness that my parents took me to church. In my adulthood, I've become aware of how fragile life is, how unpredictable it is, and my ever-present need for the grace of God. I've learned that church and Christians are for the most part imperfect and disappointing, but a necessary part of our lives in order to grow and help each other.

Growing up, I was taught that if I did the right thing and followed God's laws, all would go right with me. I learned that not only is it not true, it isn't even scriptural. God promises in His word that there will be difficult times ahead, especially for believers.

One thing I have come to know through life's exciting, unpredictable, and at times painful journey is that God's grace is sufficient. His strength is more than you'll ever need. You will feel His presence in the depths of despair. There is joy and laughter in the middle of the greatest storms of life. I'm grateful for parents who introduced me to Him at a young age.

While my childhood was great and my future full of hope, I learned soon after I married my first husband that so much of life was out of my control. I've learned how to deal with the heartbreak of addiction, infidelity, and divorce. I've struggled with single-parenting two daughters, one of which was hyperactive and later developed an eating disorder and drug addiction, all of which nearly broke my heart beyond repair.

I wish to share some of my journey with you in hopes that you'll feel that you are not alone. In some way, I hope that putting this down on paper will help you, and maybe even give you some hope. Much has been taken from me over the years—hopes, dreams, a marriage, and money—but I have never lost my faith or sense of humour. I believe God gave me the gift of laughter, as promised in His word:

> . . .and provide for those who grieve in Zion—to bestow on them a crown of beauty instead of ashes, the oil of gladness instead of mourning, and a garment of praise instead of a spirit of despair. They will be called oaks of righteousness, a planting of the Lord for the display of his splendour.

—Isaiah 61:3

chapter two
LOST DREAMS

HOME VIDEO IS A WONDERFUL THING. YOU CAN WATCH THE MOVIE OF your choice and at your own convenience. You can even watch your favourite parts over and over, or fast-forward the unfavourable parts. I've often said, "Wouldn't it be fun if God put our lives on video and gave us a copy? We could put it on fast-forward and see what our lives are like five years down the road." Had I known what my life was going to be like ahead of time, I wouldn't have wanted to live to face my future. I'm so glad only God knew what was ahead for me, and that He knew I would survive.

My dreams were simple ones. I wanted a husband, two kids, maybe a dog, and a nice, modest home. Although my dream began with a picture perfect wedding, it quickly started to crumble. It's funny how we grow up to believe that if we're good people and do our best, bad things won't happen to us. I really believed that being a good Christian was a guarantee that such things would never happen to me. I had all the answers, or so I thought.

Maybe it's the Cinderella stories we hear as little girls, or the movies we shed our tears over, that cause us to believe that finding the right person in our lives means happily-ever-after. In the real world, too often our happily-ever-after dreams end in abuse, betrayal, and devastation. It's even more difficult when you've grown up to believe that being a Christian means suffering no pain. The Bible warns us not to be surprised when we go through fiery trials but to rejoice and be exceedingly glad.

In this you greatly rejoice, though now for a little while you may have had to suffer grief in all kinds of trials.

—I Peter 1:6

How does one rejoice when you find out the man you love has been unfaithful, or when you lose a child to cancer?

If we look at the word "rejoice," we might find that what the Bible is saying here is to return to our source of our joy. We live in a cruel and wicked world full of disappointments and shattered dreams, but we serve a God who's greater than any curve the enemy might throw our way. I was surprised I had to face the end of my marriage and that I would be raising my two daughters on my own, but as I worked through the pain and grieved the loss of my dreams, I got to know my God in a way I never knew Him before. I found out that He is my best friend, my comforter, my healer, my companion, my husband, my God. When I weep, He weeps with me; when I hurt, he hurts also.

My real source of joy comes from my heavenly father. I've learned how God can be my joy when all things around me are falling apart.

Placing our hopes and dreams in this world will always be disappointing, because life is so unpredictable and we are so human. I once heard it said that life is the thing that happens on the way to your dreams. How true that is! But losing our dreams doesn't mean that we stop living. We can experience joy in the middle of sorrow if we firmly hold tight to that Unseen Hand.

• • •

I wrote this a couple of years after my first marriage ended, the marriage to the father of my children. At the time, I was the only one among my friends who had gone through a divorce. Now I'm surrounded by close friends and family who are facing the same things I've had to face. I felt so alone then and believed there must be truly something wrong with me for this to have happened.

One of the most depressing things I ever did was take a drive one day through the old neighbourhood I lived in as a teen. My youngest daughter, Melissa, had an appointment in Toronto and I had a couple of hours to kill. It took me a while to actually find the street, because everything had changed so much. I finally saw my best friend's former home and I pulled my car to the side of the road and sat there for I don't know how long. A flood of memories came back to me of a less complicated time. I remembered a time of innocence and of dreams of my future, and there I sat, all my dreams crushed behind me. Life hadn't turned out at all like I'd planned.

I married when I was just twenty years old, the same age as my husband. We thought we knew it all. We were so innocent in our hopes and dreams. I recall well his extreme jealousy and insecurities, but I truly believed that when we were finally married his insecurities would be gone. I thought he would finally be secure in knowing that I was his. I didn't expect for him to cheat on me. When it all started,

I knew it in my heart and in my gut. Not even six months into our marriage, the affairs began.

Unfortunately, he suffered from addictions. Though we tried for some time to make it work, in the end we went our separate ways. We sometimes pass down to our children hereditary traits, and addiction is one of those things, like blue eyes, height, and other physical characteristics. My daughter Ashley has the addiction gene in her, and it has become my greatest challenge.

chapter three

TRUSTING A SILENT GOD
may 2, 2012

TODAY IS MAY 2... McHAPPY DAY AT McDONALDS. AS I LISTEN TO the ads on the radio about buying a Big Mac, and various other items to support McDonalds charities, not only am I craving a Big Mac, I'm reminded of a life-changing moment I had while sitting in a McDonalds long ago. Well, the lesson started at McDonalds anyway. Nevertheless, it's a lesson learned I will never forget.

When my girls were in junior and senior kindergarten, our family was falling apart. Every day was filled with the unknown and stress beyond anything my journey into adulthood had prepared me for. I wasn't the person then that I am now. I was a beaten-down, scared, insecure woman who had never even paid a bill on her own. With the help of a good Christian counsellor, I gathered the strength and wisdom to leave an unhealthy situation.

On weekends, I travelled with my daughters from London to Hamilton to stay with my parents while shopping for a home in Brantford, where I would eventually move. I was thrilled to have found an affordable semi-detached home in my preferred neighbourhood. What should have been an easy, straightforward transaction ended up taking much longer than usual. I was exhausted, stressed, and anxious to get my girls into their school on Monday so I could rest and have some peace and quiet. There wasn't anything I wanted more in that moment. I remember sitting in a McDonalds and cursing God under my breath while having an internal dialogue with Him.

I believe in letting God know when I'm angry, even if it's at Him. He knows anyway. I confessed my anger to Him, crying out, "Why couldn't You have made this one thing go smoothly? Does everything right now have to be so extremely difficult?" I felt like I was all alone and God was silently ignoring me. I felt abandoned by Him. I soldiered on and ended up having to stay with my parents for another day. By late Monday, the house transaction was complete and I was able to head home. I didn't get my Monday afternoon off as I had hoped, but I looked forward to the next day.

On Tuesday afternoon, I took the girls to school, as per usual, savouring the coming afternoon I'd have to myself. When I reached the classroom door, I was greeted by both teachers, who immediately took me aside. They proceeded to tell me that on Monday my estranged husband had come to pick the girls up from school. It was obvious to them that he had been drinking. When he told the teachers that he was there to pick up the girls, because I had been in an accident, the teachers knew this was a lie; I hadn't even brought the kids to school that day.

I was stuck in a McDonalds, cursing my Lord and Saviour.

Yes, God was silent, but He was also hard at work protecting us all. I saw God's handiwork in my being delayed in Hamilton an extra day. I knew He ignored my frustration and anger and had done what was necessary to keep us all safe. I knew going forward that we would all be okay. Whenever faced with difficult situations, and there have been many, I recall this day and what I learned.

That day, I had to call the police. I had to remove the kids from school immediately and move into my parents' home in Hamilton until my house closed in Brantford. I thought it was also interesting, though not an accident, that my choice of home came fully equipped with a security system—and trust me, it wasn't the kind of home or neighbourhood where security systems were needed.

Many times since, I've felt God's silence and experienced my own frustration. Instead I chose to trust that He was busy at work. It doesn't mean I always get what I want, but in the end I know He is bigger than anything that comes my way, and that whatever may come, His grace is sufficient to see me through.

> *Don't worry about anything; instead, pray about everything. Tell God what you need, and thank him for all he has done.*
>
> —Philippians 4:6, NLT

> *Trust in the Lord with all your heart; do not depend on your own understanding. Seek his will in all you do, and he will show you which path to take.*
>
> —Proverbs 3:5–6, NLT

> *He makes wars cease to the ends of the earth; he breaks the bow and shatters the spear, he burns the shields with fire. "Be still, and know that I am God; I will be exalted among the nations, I will be exalted in the earth." The Lord Almighty is with us; the God of Jacob is our fortress.*
>
> —Psalm 46:9–11

chapter four

ALONE

As a mom, take a journey with me for a moment and think about your worst day. A day when you weren't feeling your best and the kids were fighting all day, getting into things and challenging your every correction. You may have even shamelessly uttered, "Just wait till your father gets home." Now close your eyes and grasp the thought that Daddy is never walking through that door ever again. That's what every day is like for a single mom. Daddy isn't coming home for whatever reason; he's not going to give you the reprieve you so desperately need. There's no break coming, whether you're sick or tired or completely fed up.

In a divorce situation, the parent whom the kids don't live with on a regular basis feels tremendous guilt, and thus often becomes the "Santa Claus" parent. When the kids go to visit, giving you the rest you desperately need, this parent showers them with gifts and outings and candy and delivers them home in a state of high energy, which can take days to bring down to a normal level, making the break you just had meaningless.

Whether because of death, divorce, or the many other unplanned reasons for being alone, the pain is the same. Very few parents set out with the plan to parent alone. I was fortunate to have a wealth of support around me, through family, friends, and my church, yet there were many moments where I felt alone.

chapter five

LITTLE BLUNDERS
november 14, 1991

IT WAS RAINING OUTSIDE, MY BANK ACCOUNT WAS EMPTY, AND IN SPITE of my threats to lose my mind, my daughters refused to get along. The pressure of single parenting this day was at an all-time high. To make the day even more special, Melissa arrived home from school with head lice, her hair down to her waist. This was the third time that month! It really made my day.

After informing the school of their inability to get this problem under control, I proceeded to the drugstore to spend another thirty dollars (felt like a hundred dollars) on treatment shampoo. Not knowing my stress level was reaching its limit, my girls fought over the blood pressure tester in the drugstore, and in the process they knocked over the cough medicine display. Oh what a day!

At home, I went about my business of disinfecting the house, which I overdid, while a steady flow of tears rolled down my face. "Oh God, why me?" I cried out.

Later that day, when it was time for Melissa to practice her one line for the Christmas concert—"Wise men today can still find Christ"—she looked up at me with great confidence. "Wise men today can still make *lice*," she said. The two of us burst into a belly laugh over her innocent mix of words. She, too, had the events of the day on her mind.

Sometimes life's day-to-day stresses can be so overwhelming that we fail to see an end in sight. It seems some of us get more than our share. Isn't it great that God has a sense of humour and gave us one, too? My daughter's blunder that day brought God's blessings into focus. This is a day I look back on and laugh about. Thank you, God, for little children!

After the girls were settled in their beds for the night, I sat down and wrote this poem:

A Single Mother's Prayer

Do you mind, oh Lord
If today I sit and cry?
The children won't behave, the bills to pay,
Today I don't want to try.

Cuts and bruises on the inside,
The pain no one can see.
Alone a mother, this surely, Lord,
Was never meant to be.

Today I'm tired
I need to rest
Tired of trying
To do my best.

Through my tears, I look around
And what do I see
These precious gifts from above,
Oh Lord, you gave to me.

In the mouths of my children
You've placed your precious voice,
For in my darkest hour
They make laughter my choice.

The silly things they do.
The cute things they say.
By your grace, they put a smile
In their mommy's day.

Help me, Lord, to remember
Not to do things on my own.
With you in my heart and by my side
I'm never really alone.

chapter six

I CAN'T IMAGINE

I'VE BEEN ASKED MANY TIMES ABOUT REGRETS. EVEN THOUGH IT HAS been so very hard raising my children on my own, I simply couldn't imagine life without them. At times, they were my heartbeat, what kept me going. My oldest child, Ashley, has had so many behaviour issues. She was diagnosed with ADHD and anxiety disorders when she was very young. It took what seemed like forever to get that under control. At one time, I actually had to have two separate babysitters because no one could handle her. On her own she was amazing and easy, but in a mix with other children she was a disaster.

Often these kids get labelled as "bad," when in reality they don't have the same ability as others to control their actions. It's the difference between wanting to slug someone who's getting on your nerves and actually crossing that line and doing it. It's very difficult for them to control that impulse. I cringe when someone calls a kid "bad," as that's something they take to heart forever. They wear that label and believe it long into adulthood. I always tried to tell Ashley she did a "bad thing" rather than calling her "bad."

The other day, I heard a story about a teacher who made a child write "I am bad" over and over. The child suffered from ADHD. I'm glad I don't know who that teacher is, or I would certainly want to give them a piece of my mind.

I don't ever regret marrying my first husband. Had I not, I wouldn't have my girls. I wouldn't trade any of the good, bad, or even ugly for anything. I would do it all over again just to have them.

I wrote this poem on a Mother's Day long ago, and I feel the same today, even after all these years of battling the pain of addiction.

SLEEPING ANGELS

Giggles and laughter
A house filled with joy
No matter the gender
A girl or a boy

Little bare bottoms
Baby powder scent
Splashing in the bath
And time well-spent

Chubby little hands
A wrinkled-up nose
Dimpled little fingers
Ten tiny toes

Cuddling close
A time to treasure

Growing up fast
The years to weather

Bumps and bruises
A tender kiss
The healing touch
A mother's lips

Safe and secure from
Fear and fright
Her loving arms
Holding them tight

Bouquets of dandelions
A worm or two
Expressions of love
Especially for you

Runny noses
Cries in the night
Sibling rivalry
Refereeing the fight

Sleeping angels
Sound and secure
The day a turmoil
How did I endure

Morning sickness
The hard-felt pain
A price so small
For what we gain

To do it all over
We surely would
A precious gift
Called motherhood

This is my favourite photo of Ashley as a young child. She is beautiful and angelic-looking. This is how I see her in my heart.

These two photos are more realistic of how life with her really was. I look at these photos and smile. I love her still. She was an awesome sleeper and eater, but when she was awake she was a hundred miles an hour all day long.

chapter seven

BROKEN

WHILE SEARCHING AND BROKEN BEFORE GOD ONE DAY, I RECEIVED A moment with Him I will never forget. I was crying my heart out, and then was reminded how He laid down His life for me. I felt Him asking me to give Him my pain and brokenness. To lay it all at his feet for Him so His death wouldn't be in vain. He didn't do that just for me. He did it for us all.

THE CROSS

While cut and still bleeding
By my bed I was knelt
Searching for an answer
It was Your presence I felt

When before my eyes I saw You
Hanging on that tree
With loving words You told me
How You died to set me free

For the first time I understood
How much You really care
You were bruised and beaten
For the pain I couldn't bear

All my broken pieces
I give to You today
For on that day You died
To pay a price I couldn't pay

For all my pain and suffering
Only You hold the key
The answer is in the cross
The cross on Calvary

chapter eight

THE WOUNDED SOLDIER

THE HEALING PROCESS IS GRADUAL. IT'S A DAILY LETTING GO OF shattered dreams, broken promises, and lost childhoods. It's bringing to the cross those things that keep us captive. The process is sometimes painful, but its rewards are growth and freedom. Freedom from anger, fear, and bondage.

Satan came to kill, steal, and destroy. Jesus came that we might have life and have it more abundantly. Life begins when we allow Christ into the most vulnerable places in our lives, when we bring to the cross those things we have no power to change.

Where we were once cut and bleeding, we are now bruised and healing. We will one day bear the scars of battle, but no longer feel the pain.

A young woman who's as close to me as a daughter recently sent me a message. It was simple but meant a lot to me: "An egg cannot be used until it is broken." She inspired me to tell my story. Letting go and laying my heartbreak at His feet has been my biggest struggle of all. I let go and take back as I get impatient with the process, but as is always the case, the more I let go, the more I feel free.

chapter nine

LOVING TOUGH

I'M TELLING MY STORY BECAUSE I KNOW I'M NOT ALONE. I'M TELLING it because I'm still living it, and writing it down is good for me. I'm writing it down in the event that doing so may help another parent who's going through the same thing. There are no promises of a happy ending or answers to real questions. There are no magic solutions to knowing how to deal with this or how to continue with everyday life. What works for one doesn't always work for another. Sometimes just knowing you aren't alone is more powerful than any answer a person can give. You are not alone.

As Ashley was coming to the other side of a very serious eating disorder, while I was just learning to breathe again and sleep through the night, while the pain in my chest was beginning to subside and the pace of my heart beginning to slow, Ashley walked across the street one night and shook hands with a boy named Shawn.

She was eighteen years old and legally an adult. Emotionally, she was an insecure fifteen-year-old, desperate to have friends. She had never had a boyfriend or smoked a cigarette. She was desperate to fit in and be accepted by her peers. She had just started back to school full-time after taking time off to recover from her eating disorder, during which time she was working and taking correspondence. Her life was just getting back on track. She began to feel comfortable with a crowd she previously wouldn't have given a second glance to. They befriended her and made her feel accepted.

It was a nice neighbourhood with young and old families, and his was the only house on the block where trouble brewed regularly. It was the house where the cops frequented, party central for several underage girls and boys. This was never a problem before, as both my daughters didn't have the slightest interest in the boys across the street. I don't know what possessed Ashley to take those few steps and enter into a friendship with the boy who would start our journey into hell.

At first she tried to tell me she would never do drugs or drink and that Shawn was harmless, even very nice, and the things people said about him were untrue. I didn't trust him, but I trusted her.

That would soon change.

The first time she got drunk was Christmas 2001. We'd had a great Christmas together, the best we'd had in a long time given her newfound health. The three of us celebrated at home with our own presents, and then we joined the rest of the family at my parents' house with great food, laughter, and presents. It was a great day, but at some point Ashley went across the street and joined in a celebration of a different sort. I didn't even realize she was gone until I heard her stumble in and throw up in the bathroom. It was obvious she was very drunk. I didn't help her, and I didn't say a word. I simply proceeded in the wee hours of the morning to tear down everything Christmas inside and outside. For me the day was ruined. I didn't want to remember that it was Christmas.

I can't tell you the horror, hurt, and fear I felt inside. I knew as her mother that family genetics, her history of obsessive compulsive behaviour, and her eating disorder meant this was a very dangerous road for her to travel. All I could think was, *Here we go again.*

While I grew up in a Christian home and personally didn't go down the rebellious route of drinking, drugs, and all the other trappings of youth, I wasn't so naïve to think teenagers don't experiment. In most cases, experimentation wouldn't be the end of the world. I had always communicated to my teenage girls, however, that experimentation could be deadly for them because of the family predisposition to becoming an addict. We had family members on both sides who had struggled with addiction.

When Ashley was in her right mind, we had a conversation about it. I reminded her that she was just coming to the other side of a very serious addiction and that this road wasn't one she should travel. I also told her that while she was an adult and could make her own choices, if she chose this road she would be traveling it without me.

Until this point, I trusted Ashley so completely that she had access to my bank card and PIN so she could pick up groceries for me and go on other minor errands. In a month's time, all that changed. She started smoking crack, lost her innocence, got drunk on a regular basis, lost her job, and began stealing from me. I felt powerless to stop it. Legally, I had no rights. She became virtually unrecognizable to me as the person I knew to be her—loving, kind, hard-working, innocent, and motivated.

It took a long time before I could actually live up to my words of her traveling this road without me. You want to believe this will pass. You want to believe their tears and apologies. You want to believe this isn't as bad as it seems, that maybe you're overreacting.

One night, we got into a huge argument. She was obviously high, all the while denying it. The anger inside me boiled over. I took her by the front of her shirt and lifted her with strength I didn't know I had, holding her against the wall, screaming at her, "What are you thinking?" I knew then that I needed help. This wasn't going to go away, and it was beyond my capabilities as a parent, let alone a single one with another teenage daughter at home to worry about.

The choice I gave her was simple: get help or get out. She made her choice, and that's when she went to live with my parents. I never thought she would do to my parents the same things she did to me. I thought this would be a good thing for her, because she had such a close relationship and respect for them. They could help get her away from her "friends."

This was my hope. I was wrong.

It didn't take long for the same things to start happening there. My parents were no better equipped than I to handle it, except for the fact that they were home during the day and could keep a better watch out for her. Even the threat of being arrested for stealing their car or forging cheques on their account didn't draw her out of her downward spiral. Her friends became the most important thing to her. She would do anything they asked, no matter who it hurt, including herself.

It's the tears and pleas for a second chance that keeps you going and gives you hope that yes, finally she gets it, finally it's over. You're kept from actually doing anything by the guilt of knowing that if you take a stand, she'll end up on the streets. How guilty did I feel knowing that my parents were now doing something that I, her own mother, could no longer do?

I remained committed to my demands that she get help if she ever wanted to move back in with me. She desperately wanted to move back in, but she remained committed to her decision to not get help. The only thing that helped me stay committed was the fact that her younger sister still lived with me, and I loved her enough to do my best to keep our home a safe and stable environment. I loved my out-of-control daughter enough to be tough enough to take a stand.

It got to where I could see the tears and listen to the pleas and not be fooled into caving in. I stopped believing her lies and being manipulated by the guilt, but I never stopped feeling the pain of watching my daughter's life spinning out of control. I've never recovered from the sense of helplessness.

Abusive boyfriends and drug dealers have come around, wanting their money. We've made trips to the courthouse and spent sleepless nights without knowing where she was. She's had bruises from fights with her so-called friends. We've seen lost dreams, jobs, lies, deception, and suicide attempts.

Things have improved over the past year, and sometimes I think it's finally coming to an end. The trauma is less, the drug use is less, but the partying continues. I know in my heart that it only takes one time. That one time she takes a bad dose of E or an overdose of cocaine. It only takes one time for someone to put something in her drink at a bar. The worry never ends.

I have emotionally and mentally prepared myself for the phone call that comes in the middle of the night, that call which brings me the worst possible news. I know that if I get that call, I will survive, but I hope and pray I never do.

THINGS I'VE HAD TO LEARN

I've learned that there's very little in life we have complete control over.

I've learned what crack, cocaine, methamphetamine, crystal meth, and E is—and what it can do to the body and mind.

I've learned that you can get a judge to give you a court order to have your adult child arrested and put into a hospital to save their life, but the hospital can ignore your efforts and let them go.

I've learned that you can sell your home and move to the other side of the city, but they'll always find a way back to where the trouble is.

I've learned how to anonymously report a drug dealer.

I've learned what crack smells like.

I've learned that without money there is very little help.

I've learned how to pray for the worst to happen so the healing can begin.

I've learned that by rescuing someone, you help the pain to continue.

I've learned that your parents don't always know what's best but their hearts are a never-ending source of love.

I've learned that as long as there are drugs in her system, the daughter I once knew doesn't exist.

I've learned that no matter how much joy comes into my life, I will always ache for the child who is lost.

I've learned how to sleep at night most of the time.

I've learned to enjoy every positive moment I have with her.

I've learned there is very little I can do for someone who doesn't want help.

I've learned that sometimes love has to be tough.

I've learned that it's not my fault.

I've learned that this is not a single-parent problem but affects families from all walks of life.
I've learned that sometimes love isn't enough.
I've learned that God's grace is sufficient.
I know that as long as there is breath, there is hope!

chapter ten

ONE TO MISSIONS, THE OTHER TO DETOX

IT WAS SOMETHING I THOUGHT AND HOPED WOULD PASS. MELISSA had wanted to do so many other things, be so many other things, I thought—and admittedly even prayed—this, too, would pass. First, she wanted to be a professional basketball player, and I suppose this could have happened easily with her 6'1" height and natural talent for the sport. However, an accident and ankle that just didn't bounce back squashed that dream, or so I thought; I would later learn it was her lack of self-confidence and insecurities that kept her from pursuing that dream. Then it was modelling and acting, and for a while that really seemed possible. With the guidance of a Christian talent agent, she got a few jobs here and there. Everyone in the industry seemed to love her and had high hopes for her. Certainly, her God-given natural beauty and slender frame meant she was made for this. That, too, slowly faded. She tried college briefly, but just couldn't settle on what it was she actually wanted to study.

Then came Youth with a Mission (YWAM). Melissa in the mission field. Now this I hadn't seen coming. This was my daughter who never strayed far from home. As a matter of fact, she got homesick quite easily, even though she was twenty years old. I won't even go into her fear of bugs and her need for luxury.

Nevertheless, this calling was on her heart for over a year before I came to the realization that she was actually going to go. Yes, I prayed it wouldn't happen. I didn't believe this was God calling her. First of all, where was Melissa going to get the money? If she really needed to find God's call on her life, why did it have to be so far away? Wasn't God here, too?

My best friend, bless her heart, was enough of a friend to give me her honest opinion. She told me that this could be the one thing that she always looked back on and wondered, "What if?"

"What a perfect time in her life to go and do this," my friend said. "It will change her in ways you can't imagine, and she will grow spiritually and emotionally in ways she couldn't do here."

I'm so thankful that I listened and decided to start praying for God to change my heart. It wasn't long afterwards that Melissa got her acceptance letter to go to YWAM in Perth, Australia, and she would be leaving in a month's time. The day she got the news, she was so excited. By the grace of God, I was excited with her and for her. He had changed my heart and given me the ability to see beyond the practicalities to what He was going to do.

Before she left, God began an enormous change in her as she said goodbye to her friends, family, and all that gave her a sense of home. I knew she was really serious when she gave up her cell phone.

We celebrated her twenty-first birthday, Thanksgiving, and Christmas in September before she left. I even decorated our home for Christmas, and we served Christmas dinner with all the trimmings. This would be the first birthday, Thanksgiving, and Christmas we wouldn't all be together.

I was so proud of her as I watched her prepare to go. I knew if it were me I would be terrified. Part of me was afraid for her, but still I felt so very peaceful and excited for her. I held my composure so well at the airport that I surprised myself. She begged me not to cry, as it would make it too difficult. It wasn't until she walked through those last doors and I could no longer see her that I turned and saw Ashley break down. Then the tears came.

There was a time when these two sisters would have never cared if the other left, but as I watched Ashley's reaction, I realized that Melissa's life had impacted her. I'm proud of Melissa simply for the fact that she's my daughter, but I'm also in awe of her life, which she allowed God to take control over. I'm in awe of how God has taken her life and not only changed it but has used it to touch others in ways she's not even aware. For years I've prayed for someone to come into Ashley's life to influence her in a positive way. I never dreamt it would be her own sister.

Melissa left on a Tuesday night. On Wednesday night, Ashley went into detox for the first time. I was just as proud of Melissa as I was of Ashley. These very different two lives were both taking huge steps in the right direction.

"I know my sister is praying for me," Ashley said as tears rolled down her face. "I can feel her prayers."

As expected, when Melissa first arrived she broke down in tears, feeling overwhelmed and tired from her journey—and incredibly homesick. I knew this would pass, and my husband reminded me how terrible I would feel if she didn't feel homesick at all. This passed by the third day she was there. I then began to get correspondence from her that reminds me of how big God really is. I so look forward to getting her emails from Australia, letting me know how she's doing.

She shared with me that because she grew up without being close to her dad, her view of God was distorted. She had completely missed God's grace, love, and gentle and trustworthy side. While in one of the services there, she saw a vision of God on His knees before her. His arms were outstretched toward her, and she was a little girl. He was calling her to run into His arms.

> *Just an update on what we've been doing/learning the past two weeks. The first week, we've been learning about the character of God, and it's amazing how much I didn't know about God. I learned a lot about His love and that He is trustworthy, which was huge for me. He's been speaking to me through so many people about how much He loves me, and it's just so amazing to think that someone could love me so much. Despite what I've have done to hurt Him, He still loves me. The second week, we learned about repentance and forgiveness, and I must say that this was a very hard week for me. God brought so much to the surface that I had just shoved down and hardened my heart to, or just forgotten about, and He wanted me to repent of it and leave it at the cross so I could come closer to Him.*

This is just the beginning of what God is doing in her life. I can't believe I ever tried to keep her from going. The finances came in, some of it from perfect strangers. He wanted her to go, and now I can see why. When I read her emails, I can hardly believe this is my little girl.

Before she left, I wrote out some simple little notes and put them throughout her things, where she would find them eventually. Here's what she wrote about that:

The morning after going to the cross, I found a note in one of my white bags from you, saying "You are special," and another one that said "I love you." I really felt that God was saying that to me as well. Just re-affirming that I am special to Him and that He loves me. It really just warmed my heart. He has spoken to me through so many people, through visions and scriptures, and it just made me realize that I am not alone, that He is always with me. When my heart breaks, His heart breaks more. He is taking me by the hand and leading me through life to green pastures and quiet waters, like Psalm 23.

Ashley has been going to church since Melissa left, which in and of itself is a miracle. The night Ashley went into detox, it was completely unknown to me. She didn't want me to know and had asked my husband and family not to tell me; she knew it would break my heart to know she was struggling with drugs once again.

That evening, I was out with two of my closest friends when I did something out of character for me. I picked up my cell phone in the middle of dinner and texted Ashley: "You know we love you right." Little did I know she was on her way to detox and I wouldn't be able to share this with her again for a while, as cell phones are not allowed. I love God moments like that.

chapter eleven

AFRAID TO BELIEVE

Ashley came to live with me while she was waiting for her apartment to be ready to move into. My heart was full of fear. I was afraid to believe this would be okay, afraid to be hurt again by lies, broken promises, and the chaos that addiction brings to a home. Nevertheless, shortly after Melissa left, Ashley moved into her room.

To say I was nervous would be putting it mildly. Nervous, scared, sceptical, stressed out, but at the same time hopeful. I've become so accustomed to the rug being pulled out from under my feet that I'm afraid to enjoy the good moments when they come, afraid to believe that change is possible, that God is in control.

I had planned a weekend away with my girlfriends, and I went, but my heart was at home, worrying that Ashley would mess up and slip back into her old ways, that chaos would return to my home.

As it turned out, the weekend at home went well. When I returned, Ashley greeted me with something she wanted to share with me. I listened to her tell me about how she lay in her room at night and realized for the first time in her life that she was indeed a good person. She told me how when she thought about all the good things about herself, she realized that Satan had bound her by that one lie (that she was bad) her whole twenty-two years. She told me how she had done a lot of bad things but that she was a good person who had been trying to destroy her own life in so many ways—her eating disorder, the drugs, the men—all because she believed a lie about herself.

In that moment, she felt the presence of God and began to remember scripture verses that she had never realized she put to memory. One in particular was Jeremiah 29:11: *"For I know the plans I have for you, says the Lord. They are plans for good and not for disaster"* (NLT). While she was telling me this, tears ran down her face. She told me that she could see how the lifestyle she had been living had been so insane.

I can't tell you how long I'd prayed for this to happen. Prayed that she would see the light. Prayed that she would see what I see, what God sees when He sees her. Now, here she was, telling me this, and yet I was scared. Thrilled on the one hand, very thrilled. In awe of how big God really is, so thankful for His grace, but still scared.

I'm scared to believe that this is the end of all the heartache. I'm scared to get close to her again for fear that she'll hurt me. Scared of being lied to, deceived again. Afraid to hope, believe, embrace a new beginning. The road to addiction is a short one, whereas the road to recovery is long and just beginning.

I've had to learn to be patient again, to embrace what she is today and take it one day at a time. She's not where I'd like her to be, but she's so far from where she once was. I am very proud.

HELP ME FORGET

Lord, help me be patient,
supportive, loving, and kind.

Help me forget yesterday
and trust in your time.

Help me, Lord, to embrace what is
And not what should be.
Help me forget yesterday
And let you set her free.

Help me let go.
Help me to rise above.
Help me to forget yesterday.
And show her your love.

Help me to be still.
Help me to be free.
Help me to forget yesterday
And let her be.

Months later, Ashley is still progressing daily. She's studying to take her GED and dating a new man. She's on her own again and enjoys visiting with us regularly just to chat, hang out, and have a free dinner here and there. In one respect, it has been great to have her sister away at this time as we rebuild our relationship. This is her time, and we're thoroughly getting to know the young woman who has been lost for so long.

Today I heard from Melissa. It's getting towards the end of her days away, and these days are the toughest. We're all longing to have her back home, safe and sound. She won't be coming home my little girl; she'll be coming home a confident young woman.

This conversation was via MSN Messenger, and I'm so thankful for the technology. It seems only a few short days ago when she called, in tears, as she was very ill. It's hard as a mom to hear that on the other end of a phone and feel so helpless. She made it through and is obviously having the time of her life.

Melissa says:	*AHHHH I'm doing awesome*
Judy says:	*excellent that is so good to hear... I pray for you every time I think of you which is lots*
Melissa says:	*aw thank you sooo much it's a French speaking country here so I really have to refresh my memory*
Melissa says:	*mom I have amazing stories to tell you*
Judy says:	*I bet you do I can't wait I'm ready for you to come home*
Melissa says:	*I danced in front of over 3000 people in a church on stage with the choir and the holy spirit was all in that place I felt I was dancing and having a party with Jesus*
Judy says:	*that is awesome*
Judy says:	*I love you so much and miss you more*
Melissa says:	*I love you soo much too oh mom guess what I live in right now*
Judy says:	*what*
Melissa says:	*it really makes you appreciate what you have we live in this motel that has a hole in the wall to the guys room lol but you can't see it unless you stick your head in and there is only 2 bathrooms for the whole place with a dribble of water that comes out for the shower lol it's sooo funny but I actually like it cause it's really adventurous*
Judy says:	*WOW... who are You? you can't be my Melissa?*

Judy says:	*this truly is a God thing because normally you would not be able to do this*
Melissa says:	*yes it truly is oh man I have to tell you how amazingly God has worked the moment we arrived here it's incredible I can't wait to tell you*
Melissa says:	*ok I love you soooooo much toooo oh man mom I'm so ready to take on anything you have no idea what I've seen and done here*

Her last comment impacted me the most. God is so good to have given her this opportunity.

When there were just thirty days until Melissa came home, I started counting the sleeps. We were all looking forward to that day and it just wouldn't come soon enough. The only person not as excited as us was perhaps Melissa herself. While she missed us, she had discovered a new home and a new love called Australia.

chapter twelve

MY LITTLE SISTER, MY ANGEL

ONE DAY DURING THIS WAITING PERIOD, ASHLEY STOPPED BY WITH A favour to ask me. She had written her sister a letter and asked me to put it in a nice format that could be framed, for her to give to Melissa when she returned.

I've read this letter over and over again, and I couldn't be more proud of both my girls. Both have been through so much together and both have overcome so much. Read Ashley's words as she talks about a little sister who was simply obedient to God's call to be there for her when no one else could.

Melissa, I can't begin to tell you how much I love you and look up to you. I have watched you mature and become, to me, a wonderful, amazing person and I'm so proud of you in so many ways.

I think that you are the most beautiful girl in the world and I tell everyone that if there was one person I would love to be like, it would be you.

Melissa, I hope you know how sorry I am for all the rough times I put you and mom through. Always standing you up when we'd make plans, and not being there for you at times when you needed me the most. There is no way I even deserve your love. Yet that day when you picked me up at Nanny's and took me to your house and I told you about everything that was going on with me and we cried together, I felt like such a failure as a sister and that was when I first decided that I was tired of my (what I thought was a happy) lifestyle and I was going to do whatever it took to change, even if it meant going for help.

It was a hard step to take but I really felt it was something I had to do. If not for myself, I was going to do it for you. I couldn't bear being your lost sister, the sister you didn't even recognize or remember. I just want you to know that you really saved my life. You believed in me, prayed for me and that alone was what gave me the willpower and determination to change.

Melissa, I love you so much and if I could tell you in one word what I feel about you and think of you, it is that you are my angel.
—Ashley, March 2008

I wrote Ashley a note on her Facebook, letting her know how proud I was of her and the letter she had written to Melissa. Her reply to me touched my heart all over again.

Aw mom, thank you so much for doing that for me. I am so happy that you and I are close again and having a relationship. I honestly have never felt so happy and alive in my life right now. This year has already turned out to be an awesome year in so many ways. I honestly would never even think of or want to go back to that awful lifestyle that completely destroyed who I was and I was so, so lost, and even hurt you guys so much. . . Thank you so much mom, that even though I hurt you and made you worry for what must have seemed for eternity, that you never stopped praying for me and you never gave up on me.

It's such a miracle, isn't it? Not so long ago, it all seemed so hopeless. So many sleepless nights, so many tears, so many prayers.

I'm so proud of my girls. They've been my heartbeat for so long. They were my reason to keep going when life seemed too hard. Together we made so many memories, memories to laugh at, to cry about, and to cherish.

Now that they are young women, I feel a sense of letting go. Their lives are still ahead of them, but I feel that my job as a mom is done, and I'm proud. I'm proud of the women they are and the women I know they are becoming. I don't know what the future holds for them, who they will marry, how many children they will have, what kind of career path they will take, but I'm certain they are both in God's hands and that the same God who brought me through my life's journey is the same God who will see them through.

chapter thirteen
IT CONTINUED

I WISH THE STORY ENDED WITH THAT LAST CHAPTER, BUT IT DIDN'T. IT got worse and then better, worse and then better.

Shortly after coming out of detox and moving out of our home and into a room at my sister's, Ashley entered into a toxic relationship. It's no mystery how or why they found each other. What is broken in her and broken in him are a perfect match for a perfect disaster. I can't tell you the number of times we have rescued her from their home only to have her go back. Words cannot express the kind of pain that inflicts on a mother's heart.

Just before Christmas one year, she suffered a painful miscarriage and we both felt relief. Sadness for what we lost, for sure, but relief just the same. We knew they weren't ready to raise a child and that the relationship was not a healthy home for any child.

One week before Melissa's wedding, Ashley told me she was breaking up and ready to leave. Two weeks following Melissa's wedding, she told us she was pregnant again. I was devastated but showed support. What could I do? Nine months later, the most precious, beautiful little boy came into our lives. Like my own children, I wouldn't trade him for anything.

Being a grandparent is the most awesome thing in the whole world, and it's our reward as parents for having children. God's reward. We get to be fun, silly, cuddle, and spoil these little bundles of joy and then give them back to the parents for discipline and to nurse through colds, coughs, and restless nights. Or at least that's the way it's supposed to be, right?

Since our grandson came into our lives, we have had him overnight at least once a week. This past year, he was in our full-time care twice. We have rescued him from the side of the road while both his parents sat in separate police cars under arrest. He lived with us for three weeks while Mommy was relapsing with a prescription overdose and Daddy was in jail. There are no words to express the pain I feel for this precious little boy who deserves so much better.

While she's doing well, Ashley is an awesome mother, and her little boy is very attached to her. For most of his life, she has been doing well. When the times are good, they are really good. When the bad times are bad, they are really bad.

I would love to get off this rollercoaster of emotion. I would love to enjoy my selfish years and empty nest. I golfed twice this past summer, and I usually golf once a week. We gave up our annual family barbecue. We gave up holidays. We gave up time together, sleep, walks at night, time with friends, and so much more. I'm in debt for childcare that wasn't in the budget, yet I would still do it all over again for this precious little boy who has stolen my heart. Each time we help, we get kicked in the teeth by the ones we helped the most.

My hope is that Ashley will get victory over her addictions once and for all, including the one she has with her toxic relationship. In a perfect world, they both would get healthy and be the parents their son so deserves. This is my prayer daily.

chapter fourteen

CANCER GAVE US A BREAK

Just when I had given up on men all together, a dear friend of mine thought I should meet Ron. "He's perfect for you," she said.

The meeting happened and I knew instantly Ron and I could be friends, but I told her he just wasn't my type. To this day, he takes that as a compliment, because in the past my type wasn't the type he would want to be identified with.

We became friends and bonded over our mutual grief of lost relationships. He had lost his wife to a very long illness and learned what it was to really love a person unconditionally. He missed her very much. I always say that he came fully trained, that I have the perfect man.

We had a long friendship before it became romantic, and that took me by surprise. When I suddenly noticed that I had real feelings for him, I wanted to run. Why he never ran, I'll never know. While he was getting to know me, my girls were at their worst. Melissa was seventeen and at an annoying teenager stage, though she was a relatively easy teen to deal with. Ashley was into her full-blown addiction and trying every drug she could get her hands on. It wasn't a pretty sight. I told Ron many times to run. His statement to me every time was "I'm not going anywhere."

My husband is perfect. First of all, he came with a housekeeper. His housekeeper had gone above and beyond for his late wife Maggie, and he'd promised her she would always have a job with him. It was a little weird at first having someone else clean my home, but I adjusted real quick. Ron is a fabulous cook, and he loves to grocery shop. He even prefers to do his own laundry. He rarely gets upset and always sees the bright side, never making a bad situation worse. He has become our rock. Most importantly, he loves my girls as though they were his own. He is a gem and I love him very, very much.

I kissed a couple of frogs before he came into my life and was treated very badly, cheated on, and yelled at. Then along came my prince. My wonderful husband, who never even complains when he's sick, came to me one day with a chronic earache he'd been nursing for what seemed like months. He said, "I'm kind of concerned, honey, because I have this lump on the side of my neck." I gasped, instantly knowing this was not good.

The day before our fifth anniversary, we got the diagnosis. The lump we had found in his neck was indeed cancer, and the treatment began immediately. This meant daily visits to the hospital for treatments.

The prognosis was good, but treatment was brutal. Think of the worst sore throat you've ever had, then imagine you can't swallow or eat for six months to a year. Think about adding on top of that third-degree burns all down the side of your neck and face. Think about having to feed yourself through a tube in your stomach and drink only liquids.

Hear me when I tell you that this man didn't complain one minute the entire time he went through all this. As a matter of fact, he was more concerned about assuring everyone else that he was okay. He wore a smile and cracked a joke to everyone he met in the hospital. Throughout this, he went from being my friend, my love, to my hero.

Cancer gave us a reprieve, because throughout this whole ordeal Ashley kept her problems from us. If she and her partner fought, we didn't hear about it. If there was something wrong, we didn't see it. What was really important came into focus.

My man is my rock, and he is most certainly heaven-sent. He says we rescued him, too, and gave him the family he never had. He loves my girls, he rejoices at their victories, and he weeps for them in hard times. It was as though they were his from the beginning. I can't imagine what I have ever done to deserve such a gift.

I'm so thankful that cancer didn't take him from us. It's so sad that it took cancer to give us the break we needed, for what came after cancer would have surely been more than we could bear.

chapter fifteen
SHE CALLED ME EVIL

It was a cry in the night, a parent's worst nightmare. It wasn't the first time, but we had hoped it would be the last. Just when Ashley was getting her life back on track and moving in the right direction, along came another toxic relationship.

This new relationship has robbed us of sleep, joy, and peace. The human in me has always wanted to strangle him and give him a piece of my mind. I admit to thinking unchristian thoughts about him and whispering unkind prayers. The Christian in me loves him like a son and has welcomed him into our home and adopted him as a family member. I've had compassion for him, for I know his upbringing wasn't like the one I so fortunately had. His was a life of disappointment and loss as a young child. No child should have to go through what he has.

I've prayed for his soul and defended his character. I've overlooked his shortcomings and forgiven him time and time again for his offences. I chose to see the good in him and believed that should God get a hold of his life he would change into the man I knew he could be. I know that in some ways he is really good for her, but in many ways he holds her back from progressing, growing, and moving in the direction she was moving before he came along.

His abusive ways are subtle and his charm can be turned on when needed. He knows the right things to say and the right times to say them. Her self-esteem and self-image are very low, so he belittles her, calling her stupid because she didn't finish high school. He says her jobs are meaningless and a waste of time instead of praising her for a job well done. She is an awesome mother and housewife, though she's told she's lazy and sits around all day.

He keeps her in a constant state of worry with all the unlawful ways in which he chooses to live. Her name is attached to his deeds, so she'll bear the consequences if caught. He keeps her financially and emotionally trapped. Before him, her goal was to return to church and begin to sing in the choir; she has a beautiful singing voice. She would love to take her son to church, but she isn't allowed so neither of them go. This breaks my heart.

In a way, this is all he knows. This is what he lived, and in some respects so has she. Though she's tried many times to leave, she continues to go back. This time we thought it was final. We had hoped, we had prayed. Things didn't go smoothly, as can be expected. The police were called and charges were laid, and all seemed as though this would be permanent.

I wasn't surprised by her change of heart, as we've been through it so many times before. I was, however, surprised by how swiftly her heart changed and how quickly she forgot all the reasons she wanted out. She had cried to get out, said she couldn't go on. She forgot all the things she told us about him and how awful it made her feel. She forgot her sense of hopelessness and despair. She forgot her disgust at some of his ways and how she so desperately wanted to be free to choose what she wanted for her son. She forgot her anger and heartbreak and the fact that she felt she could never trust him.

We offered her freedom, a place to live. We offered excellent legal help, money to get started on her own, and anything else she needed. We offered to do whatever it took to get her out of the situation. We desperately wanted her to just be okay. The sacrifices we had to make would have been nothing in comparison.

But instead she turned her back on us and decided to return to the sadness she had desperately tried to escape. It's her life. She called me "evil." Evil, because I wouldn't agree; evil, because I didn't approve; evil, because I wouldn't do what my conscience wouldn't allow. I was asked to help. I helped, I loved, I sacrificed, I gave, and I am "evil."

I'm told it's normal for a woman to turn on those who love her most, but somehow it doesn't help me. I am wounded, I am broken, I am grieving. I can't unknow what I now know. I can't unhear what I've heard or forget what I've seen. I know I will go on by the grace of God, but a huge part of me is missing as long as she is lost. My friend put it best: "It's as though your heart is wandering around outside your body."

My sleep is filled with nightmares, my hope is lost, my despair is great. Will I ever forget? Will I heal, will this end? How do I watch them marry? How do I watch them together? How do I go forward, knowing, knowing, knowing what lies beneath, and what lies ahead?

• • •

There always seems to be that boyfriend, girlfriend, or friend whom our loved one needs to get away from to get better. I hear it over and over again. The truth is that it's easier for us to blame the obstacle, the enabler, and the bad influence than it is for us to blame the decision-maker: our loved one, our child. The reality is that, yes, they may be surrounded by negative influences, but unless and until our loved one takes ownership of their choices and begins to make healthy ones, they will always find another obstacle, bad influence, or enabler. It will never be possible for us to build a shield around them, but there is hope as long as they engage in all the help that's at their feet. It's their choice, their responsibility.

chapter sixteen

I LET GO...
AND IT GOT WORSE

THE DAY GOD FINALLY GOT THROUGH TO ME AND I FINALLY LET GO of Ashley and completely put her in His hands, I knew things would likely get worse. Because of decisions they had made together and the path they were on, they could get arrested—or worse. Nevertheless, I let go because I knew it was the right thing to do. It was my only option.

I could hear the sigh of relief in heaven, and all heaven rejoiced at my decision to finally live my life in the comfort and peace that God was bigger than what lay ahead. I began to enjoy life again and all that I had been missing. I enjoyed spending time with old friends and building new relationships. For the first time since Ashley had come home drunk on Christmas night so many years ago, I embraced Christmas. I was overwhelmed by the presence of peace, though the storm raged on in her life. I had decided that though the devil may have her at present, he wasn't going to have me as well. So I lived.

•   •   •

At the sound of Ron's voice on the other end of my work phone, I knew something had happened. "It's Ashley," he said. "It's real bad."

I thought he was going to tell me she was gone. I braced for what was to come next. Ron was in tears on the other end of the line as he began to tell me what had happened.

Drugs had taken over her life once again. Though we had suspected as much, we hadn't been certain. Now we knew. In an overdose that should have taken her life, Ashley lost control and drove her car off the road (the car I had gifted to her just a short time before). She then proceeded to throw herself into traffic over and over. A truck driver managed to stop to avoid hitting her. She was then put into the hospital under a seventy-two-hour hold. I don't like to think about that day or what could have happened. This was bad. All kinds of questions came to mind about her future—our little precious grandson's future. His daddy faced court and possible jail the next day for a previous charge. Would Ron and I suddenly become full-time parents again?

A day later, I saw Ashley, though she wasn't coherent nor did she look like my daughter. A mess. She was a mess. This was a mess. Was there hope? It didn't look good… but still I felt peace. I heard God's voice saying, "I've got this… I've got this."

She left rehab and walked into the waiting arms of her Lord and Saviour… and emerged the daughter I'd lost so long ago. There isn't a Sunday in church when I don't wipe tears from my cheeks, as she hasn't missed a Sunday since. I think I know a little of how God must feel when a lost one comes home. I don't care what she's done in the past or the things she has said. None of it matters. I'm overwhelmed with pride for who I see her becoming.

For someone recovering from addiction, her situation is less than ideal—hopeless, some might say—but she's facing it and dealing with it one day at a time, embracing everything God has placed in her life to help her. New friends, counsellors, teachers, books and prayer are her weapons against the things that try to bring her down. Her faith wasn't shared by her partner, nor were the two of them on the same page about their son attending church. This was a weekly battle. One day, while she expressed her concerns about how her son's future would look given this difference of opinion between them, I said to her, "It isn't about a perfect family or perfect situation. It's about a perfect God. He's got this."

The conversations we have now are amazing. I cannot believe how far she's come in such a short time. I'm enjoying every minute of having her back, knowing this could all go wrong so easy. Addiction is resistant to change and subject to relapse, so I know how quickly it could all go away. She's going to make it if she continues to hold on tight to that Unseen Hand. She went into detox broken and emerged with new hope and a brand new start. I love her so deeply and I'm deeply proud.

The hardest thing for a mother to do is let go of her child and really trust God to see them through. Over dinner one evening, my friend told me about her worries over her son in university who wasn't serving God. She was so concerned about his future. From my perspective, I smiled and said, "Trade ya." He was a fine young man who was studying hard and going places. Yes, he was off-track a little spiritually and dabbling in drinking, but in comparison it could have been so much worse. After I said this, she looked at me and said, "Yes, but it only takes one bad night of drinking and his life could be lost forever."

Another friend shared that when she was a young teenager, she'd lived a godly Christian life. That is, until she met one guy who took her off-track for a time. Another near and dear friend had a precious little three-year-old girl who died suddenly. While it had been over twenty years since that loss, you could still see a tear in her eye at the mention of her name. Her life had gone on, and though she struggled through many of life's twists and turns, she maintained a strong grip on God's hand throughout the journey.

Why did it take so long for me to truly let go and experience God's peace? I curled up in the fetal position on my bed every time things weren't right with her. I ceased to live in spite of the fact that God had been there for me in so many difficult situations. Why did I have such a hard time truly trusting Him with this one?

I reflected on a journey I once made to a women's conference with a group of mothers, getting away for a weekend. On the journey, we talked about the best thing that had happened in our lives, and we all agreed that having our children was the best. Then we began to share about the worst things. One shared that losing their child was the worst thing. Another shared that being molested by a trusted loved one was the worst thing. Still another shared that finding out her husband was molesting their daughter was the worst thing she had to endure. A fourth woman shared that when she and her husband had to move their family out of province because of his job, that was her worst thing.

Though no one spoke it, I was thinking it. I'm sure others were, too. "Trade ya." I remember that conversation so vividly. It speaks to me. So often we feel we get more than our share while others suffer in this world so little. So it seems. As I ponder this, though, I think it's all the same. I think it's all relative, all painful, no matter what it is. The key is the same in all—we have to let go. Whatever happens, we have to trust God to work in that situation. It's not just me who struggles with this. We all do, on some level, because we're human. For me, being a single mom, my girls meant the world to me. They were my heartbeat in the midst of trying to make everything work for us. I think that's why it was so very hard for me to let go of my girl. My firstborn.

I'm looking at a situation that doesn't hold a lot of hope, except for the fact that now God is in the midst of it.

Two verses Ashley sent to me by text the other day were:

But you, O Lord, are a shield around me; you are my glory, the one who holds my head high.

—Psalm 3:3, NLT

The Lord himself will fight for you. Just stay calm.

—Exodus 14:14

chapter seventeen

...AND THEN IT WAS OVER

ASHLEY GOT SO BRAVE. WITH THE HELP OF HER COUNSELLOR AND PEER support worker, she made a plan to leave her partner. She packed her bags and her son's and was going to stay with us until she could get a place of her own. She sat on my couch and said, "Mom, if I go back this time, I won't make it."

She went back the next day.

I remember vividly the morning she went back. It was a Sunday morning and we had all planned on going to church as per usual. She entered my room that morning and said, "I'm not going." I could see it in her face and in her stance. She had changed overnight. She had gone back to the way she had been. Without warning, the cycle began again.

She left to go see him and asked me to take our grandson to church. I'll never forget her son screaming at the top of his lungs at the top of our stairs: "Mommy, I want to go to church. Come back, come back!" I had never heard him cry like that before. I will always wonder what might have been different had she turned around that morning and took her son to church.

I don't know how I managed to comfort him, but I calmly told him that Grandma would take him to church. He calmed down and somehow we went about the business of getting ready.

Weeks later, we got a call from Melissa in the middle of the night. Ashley had overdosed again. On a gut feeling, Melissa and her husband had gone out to check on her—and saw her passed out through the window. They called 911 and the paramedics were able to get her out of her unconscious state and take her to the hospital.

She survived, but every day I hear her words: "If I go back this time…"

The Ashley who emerged from this experience is one I don't recognize. The things that come out of her mouth are so cruel, I can't repeat them. Fortunately, our grandson was with us when this happened and Daddy was in jail serving a short sentence for repeat traffic offences. Our grandson was placed in our care by the Children's Aid Society (CAS), and he celebrated his third birthday with us, without either parent present. There are no words for how we felt about that.

Every morning when I received an angry text from Ashley, I was just thankful she had made it through the night and was still alive. It doesn't matter how often a person is arrested and placed on a seventy-two-hour hold, the hospital here lets a person go within hours even if they are clearly a danger to themselves.

Two weeks later, we had to hand our grandson back to his dad. I've developed a new respect for the workers at CAS whose hands are tied. They have to give a parent every opportunity to change before they can take them away. Ashley isn't allowed to parent at the moment, and neither are they allowed to parent together. Though we've been promised all kinds of change, we've heard it all before.

chapter eighteen
EVERY DAY IS A CHOICE

EVERY DAY IS A CHOICE. A CHOICE NOT TO GO TO A PLACE OF ANGER. A choice not to go to a place of hate. Sometimes every hour is a choice, even every minute.

Ashley called me "Evil." She called me worse, words I cannot repeat, nor will I likely ever forget. I don't know what kind of apology will ever take those words away from a mother's heart. I can forgive the drugs, I can forgive the deceit, I can forgive the anger, I can forgive the pain, but I struggle daily with the choice she has made over us. The choice to stay with the one addiction she has yet to free herself from—and that is her partner.

I've taken the blame for what I haven't done, for words I haven't spoken, in order to keep peace. I don't understand. I cannot comprehend why. If it weren't for my little grandson, I believe I could walk away. I'm tired and exhausted.

I grieved for a long time. I'm so thankful for a husband who allowed me to grieve and never required anything more from me than I was able to give. I told him, "If she goes back, I don't think I'll make it this time." All he said was, "I know." Nothing more. Yet those were the most comforting he could have spoken. He gave me permission to grieve, to fall apart, to just be human. Most importantly, in those words I heard him say that he would understand and love me anyway. I felt that same kind of love and understanding from my heavenly father. He knew.

I did grieve, and in one of my darkest moments God spoke to my heart. I realized that if I stayed in this state, Ashley's addiction and the evil behind it would get a two-for-one deal. It would take both me and my daughter, and everything that was left of my family. I love a good bargain, but this was a deal I wasn't willing to make. Determination rose up in me I didn't know I had. Fire began to burn in my soul to rise above this and not let it beat me.

I realized, too, that I had been unfair to my daughter, who clearly struggled to manage everyday life. Her need to self-medicate was stronger than the invaluable treasures in her life. On top of what she already found too much to bear, I was placing my own happiness in her hands. I was adding my well-being to her long list of worries, guilt, and regrets. I needed to allow God to dig me out of this pit and allow Him to be my source of joy, my source of comfort, to let go of everything in her that was completely out of my control.

Letting go was gradual, not easy, but life-changing. I chose to leave my house. I chose to make new friends. I chose to go to church and to sing a little louder and praise Him a little stronger. My feelings followed what I chose to do. In church, tears streamed down my face uncontrollably. It was embarrassing, but I chose to go anyway. I soon began to feel joy instead of pain. I found myself looking forward to Christmas again. I found myself accepting invitations to go out with others and build new friendships. I found myself learning to live with the sadness that had once overshadowed everything.

I found myself enjoying a deeper, richer relationship with Melissa and my perfect husband Ron.

I began to forgive the one I found hardest to forgive. The relationship Ashley had chosen over us. It was easy to blame others in her life as being the ones to keep her lost and broken, but in reality she was the one who needed to get healthy and make good choices. Otherwise she would just find another broken person to share her life with. The faces would change, but the cycle would be the same. Problems existed long before her current partner had. He had his part in it, but he was not to blame for it.

I forgave him and added him to my prayer list. First thing in the morning and last thing at night, I prayed for all three of them.

One Sunday, our pastor said, "Bitterness is like drinking a cup of poison and expecting the other person to get sick." Forgiveness was for me a step towards letting go of what would make me sick if I didn't. Though the forgiveness may never be returned or appreciated, doing so sets me free.

Everything Ashley and her partner have been through has forced them into the help they've always needed. As long as they continue to engage in that help, there's hope for them all. Even though I hated him for the choices he made and the choices she made because of him, he's the one she listened to when she decided to go to rehab. He and her son were the reasons she had gone, and for that I can be thankful. Very thankful.

Every once in a while, we get a glimpse into the ways in which God works behind the scenes, protecting and reaching each one us. Those glimpses remind me that He's got this, that He's doing what I cannot. Short of crawling up inside her and controlling her decision-making buttons, there's nothing I can do. God won't take a person's free will, but He will put people and things into their lives to reach them and draw them closer to what's best for them.

> *Then Jesus told them this parable: "Suppose one of you has a hundred sheep and loses one of them. Does he not leave the ninety-nine in the open country and go after the lost sheep until he finds it? And when he finds it, he joyfully puts it on his shoulders and goes home. Then he calls his friends and neighbors together and says, 'Rejoice with me; I have found my lost sheep.'"*

—Luke 15:3–6

THANKFUL (WRITTEN ON THANKSGIVING DAY, 2013)

I am thankful for my two daughters, whom I couldn't imagine my
     life without.

I am thankful for my awesome grandson, who delights me more
     each day.

I am thankful for the most wonderful husband any woman could ever
     hope for.

I am thankful for every hardship and every valley in my life, for they
     caused me to grow in ways I could never have imagined.

I am thankful that in times of heartache and sadness, I've experienced
     God's grace, joy, and peace in unforgettable ways.

Though today my heart aches for the empty seats around the table, and
     though every routine check-up reminds me that my husband's
     cancer could someday return, I am thankful.

Above all else, I am thankful that all these gifts I hold dear come from
     the same God who holds each and every one of them in the palm
     of His hand.

chapter nineteen

LETTING GO OF THE PILLOW

Loving a child who's an addict requires some really tough calls. Loving an addict means that we have to sometimes do the last thing we ever hope to do. We set our boundaries and believe and hope those boundaries will never be crossed.

My husband and I attend a family support group, and our group leader puts it very well. She says that an addict is someone who's continually banging their head against the wall; they may even be bleeding and it hurts, yet they keep doing it over and over. Then along comes a family member who puts a pillow between the addict and the wall, which softens the blow. The family member's life becomes all about holding that pillow in place to protect their loved one. In fact, the pillow keeps them from feeling the pain they need to feel in order to get help.

Loving and helping an addict is really the opposite of how you would love anyone who's suffering from any other issue. An addict has to fall hard in order to really seek help. Very few addicts go for help without suffering severe consequences first.

I was put in a position to make a very tough call, but I had to do it in order to protect Ashley and my grandson. It meant that for a time she lost her son, but it also meant she had to go to rehab to get him back.

As I write this, she has been sober for over four months. This weekend, she's moving back in with her son and the father. The cost is that she's chosen to no longer be in a relationship with me and may never be. She's alive, her son's alive, and for now that's a price worth paying. They are both getting help.

We often have to get to a place where we're so tired and exhausted from holding the pillow in place that we have to let go and let them fall—and fall hard. Maybe, just maybe, the healing can then begin. If not for them, for us. Sometimes it means making tough calls, because consequences are huge motivators—the key to recovery. My love for her life had to be more important to me than my need for her to love me back.

I didn't give up or give in, I let go of what I cannot change. I had to accept that the worst could happen and much of it would be out of my control. By learning to let go, I became determined not to allow what I had no power to change have power over me.

And then God changed me.

chapter twenty

A SILENT NIGHT

christmas, 2013

IT WAS SILENT, THOUGH NOT UNEXPECTED. THERE ARE USUALLY AT LEAST ten people gathered around the carefully decorated table. This year, we didn't exchange gifts the way we normally do. It was just me and my man in the silent house on Christmas Day. I cooked upstairs while he created a fort downstairs, a gift for our grandson's next visit. We didn't get to see him on Christmas Day, but we did get a phone message from him that warmed our hearts. Months later, it's still on our phone.

It's been months since I had a conversation with Ashley. I receive the odd text from her, just to say thank you for a gift we gave her, but my text always comes long after everyone else in the family receives theirs. It's tough to hear Ashley's silence, but I realize deep down that it's for the best right now for both of us. She needs to heal on her own and individualize from me. I'm told it's the shame that keeps her away, but I feel as though she blames me for all this.

I'm torn when I hear that she's in contact with others, like Ron and Melissa, but mostly I'm torn by the relationship she has with my mother. I'm glad she reaches out to her grandparents, but it's a painful reminder that she doesn't reach out to me. I've lost her again, and though I've been through this many times before, it never gets easier.

This time I know it's for a very long time. Truth be told, I wouldn't know what to say or how to act if she did want to talk to me. I'm so afraid of doing or saying the wrong thing.

I didn't expect a "Merry Christmas," but I slept with my cell phone by my side in hopes that there might be one. I vowed not to reach out anymore and to protect myself from further hurt, but I couldn't help putting that one present under the tree. A simple gift, a photo of her son that my husband delivered to her. Two days after Christmas, I got that "Thank you." Not a "Merry Christmas" or "I miss you" or even an "I love you," but it was something and I cherished it.

THE SOUND OF SILENCE

Your silence is deafening,
and pierces my soul.
I will endure it forever, if
it helps make you whole.

They tell me, they say
its birthplace is shame.
My heart cannot grasp why
then, it feels like blame.

The sound is hollow,
and awakens my sleep.
It beats loud in my head,
and in my stillness I weep.

It is stealing time,
laughter and healing.
And still I cannot escape,
this love I'm feeling.

My hope rests in Him
and what I cannot see.
He's the only one who can truly
set you and me free.

chapter twenty-one

WAITIN' ON A MIRACLE

AFTER I WROTE THE LAST LINE TO "THE SOUND OF SILENCE," I REALIZED that all these years I've been praying, hoping, and waiting for a miracle for my daughter, but I failed to realize that I needed a miracle as much as she did.

What we go through as mothers and family members of addicts is more than our hearts can endure. We live in a perpetual state of grief. Our children are the first thoughts on our minds in the morning and our last thoughts as we lay our heads down at the end of the day. These thoughts and sadness steal our sleep, and our only focus is on our child who is lost.

Yes, I needed a miracle just as much as she did.

Something has changed in me since the New Year. Before the end of the year, God showed me the vast need of other Christian mothers who are waiting on a miracle for their child. Most of them suffer in silence, afraid to admit to their friends, family members, and church community what they're going through. Many of us have had the police at our doors, we're raising our grandchildren, we've had drug dealers at our doors looking for money, and we've dealt with government agencies we never knew existed. It's all so much to navigate while our hearts break apart.

Our children, in the process of their addiction, do despicable things, and their behaviour strikes a path of destruction straight through the middle of our homes and our hearts. They've called us names we cannot repeat, yet if we could escape the love we feel for them none of this would matter. But we cannot. Our hearts break for them and we bleed for all the things they have lost, and none of it matters to them. All that matters to them is their drug of choice. This can change and they can be restored, but we cannot do it for them.

We cannot chose freedom for them, but we can chose to walk in freedom ourselves. This is hard, but it is possible. It means truly trusting in a God we cannot see. It means stepping aside and falling into the arms of Jesus. Even if I don't get the miracle I want so desperately for my child, I can choose the miracle waiting for me. I know that I've done everything humanly possible to save her. I know she has all the necessary tools at her fingertips in order to be successful, but whether she reaches out or not will always be up to her.

I choose life for myself. The sadness will always be there. I will always shed a tear at a memory, or a song that speaks to me, but I'll live and laugh and enjoy all that's special and present in my life. One of my favourite things about our family, immediate and extended, is our ability to laugh at almost anything. We find humour in absolutely everything, and boy do we love to laugh. I love it when we sit around and talk about old times and laugh about the things that once made us cry. I lost my laughter for a time, but it's back now. I look forward to the day when we can all be in the same room again and laugh till our bellies hurt.

chapter twenty-two
MY NEW FRIEND, JOSEPH

Our family has been hit by a tornado called addiction. It didn't come, rip our house apart, leave, and never come back. It keeps returning over and over again. We rebuild and it returns. Words cannot express the heartache this causes, the sense of loss and hopelessness.

In the middle of all this, I made a new friend and his name is Joseph. My husband and I were driving home from church one Sunday and I heard a quote from a new book on the Christian radio station. I knew instantly that I had to get my hands on that book. It was written by one of my favourite Christian authors, Max Lucado, and its title is *You Will Get Through This: Hope and Help for Your Turbulent Times.* How fitting is that?

I expected a how-to, but what I got was the inspiring story of Joseph. While it's one of my favourite stories in the Bible, it means so much more to me now. I see beyond the Technicolor dreamcoat and the delightful musical that it has become. I've had the privilege of enjoying it on more than one occasion. This story is my story. *Our* story.

What struck me most was the time in which it took for this whole story to unfold, and how much of it I could relate to. God gave Joseph a dream, a vision for his future, just like he gave me a dream for my children. There was family dysfunction, betrayal, jealousy, anger, and unjust accusations… all of which we experience as a family. In the end, there was reconciliation, which is always God's plan. But again, what struck me most over and over was time.

I confess that time is probably my worst enemy. I'm impatient and I want so badly for the pain to end. As a mother, I want to fix it and go to rescue. My humanness sometimes gets in the way of God's handiwork. I get impatient with God's work and step in and try to do it myself. As I read through Mac Lucado's book, I was impressed by Joseph's steadfastness and his calm. Things got better for him, and then worse, and then better, and then worse, over and over, yet he held tight to God's promises.

Letting go of this situation is one of the hardest things to do, but it has been life-changing. As I read, it was confirmed to me that letting go is the right thing to do, but what I newly accepted is that it will take time for healing to happen. It most certainly may not go the way I expect it should. It could take years, as it did in Joseph's life and in the life of his family.

The last two chapters of Lucado's book say it all: "Stay Calm, Go On" and "Evil.God.Good." The final chapter ends like this:

> *Trust God. No really trust him. He will get you through this. Will it be easy or quick? I hope so. But it seldom is. Yet God will make good out of this mess. That's his job.*[1]

---

1 Max Lucado, *You Will Get Through This: Hope and Help for Your Turbulent Times* (Nashville, TN: Thomas Nelson, 2013), Kobo edition.

God is in our mess. The signs are all around me. He's in the grandmothers he has brought into my life who are going through the same thing. They make me feel not alone. Normal even. They understand like others cannot.

God is in the timing that has protected our grandson from feeling the direct hit of his mother's addiction. He's in the bringing home of my daughter Melissa and her husband from their mission trip a month early so they could be here to save her life and hold my hand. He's in the support from our friends and their prayers. He's in the calm I feel when the storm rages. He's in the lives of those who know Him and have been brought into Ashley's life. He's in the fact that though the drugs should have taken her from us, she still lives today.

I feel a certain kinship towards Joseph now, and I'm inspired by how a story written so long ago is so relevant today in my own personal life. But isn't that the real awesomeness of God's word? It's so relevant, life-changing, and inspirational, no matter how often we read it. It's truth and life to us all.

chapter twenty-three

DOES EVERYTHING HAPPEN FOR A REASON?

WHENEVER I HEAR SOMEONE SAY "EVERYTHING HAPPENS FOR A reason" I have to bite my tongue. Sometimes I'm successful, but most times I just have to say something.

My husband and I used to do background acting in Toronto. This was something we kind of fell into. It was fun, so we did it whenever time allowed and earned a little extra money on the side. We've been in films and TV shows together like *Red*, *The Vow*, *The Firm* (TV series), *Covert Affairs*, and many others. My husband's claim to fame is that he played a murdered cop in a made-for-TV movie and spent many hours in a body bag being wheeled down a hill. My claim to fame is my one and only close-up, in a TV docudrama where I played a diseased street person. I'll never forget when the director said, "Release the rats." Yes, there were actual rats, though trained by a professional rat wrangler. Nevertheless, rats.

When working on set for twelve hours or more, it's a lot of hurry up and wait. There are many hours spent sitting around tables and talking to people you've never met before. Some conversations are very interesting, some are very strange.

I'll never forget one day sharing a table at the prestigious Royal York Hotel in downtown Toronto for an on-location shoot for *Covert*

Affairs. We were all dressed in glamorous gowns and tuxedos. To my left was a young woman in her twenties. She was a very sweet girl and I enjoyed talking to her all day. Then she said, "Everything happens for a reason."

I tried, but couldn't bite my tongue. "You know, I really hate that saying."

She looked at me, kind of puzzled, and asked, "Why?"

"If I were to believe that, I would have to believe that little children are molested for a reason, or little children get cancer for a reason, and I just don't believe in a God that would be that cruel. I believe we live in a world with many broken people, and bad things do happen to those who don't deserve it." I went on to tell her that I believe in a God who can take that which was meant to destroy and turn it around for good. Our wounds can be healed and make us stronger, and we can go on to help others. I believe there's no reason God would allow a child to be hurt. I believe that some things in life happen to move us in another direction, and that some things happen because of choices we make and so on.

She listened carefully. Then this young lady I'd not met before turned and thanked me. "As a child, I was molested and felt it had happened for a reason, and no one has ever said that to me before."

I'm passionate about this for that very reason. I've spent years trying to figure out what I had done to cause my divorce. I found reasons to blame myself and take ownership of what was someone else's consequences. I was deep in guilt for what was happening in my daughter's life. What did I do as a mother? What didn't I do? What was the reason this was happening? What was God trying to tell me? Guilt is a very deep pit to get out of.

"Everything happens for a reason" keeps many of us captive. I was stuck for a long time in a cycle of trying to fix something that wasn't mine to fix, to learn some lesson I thought God was trying to teach me in all this. Oh, there are many things I have learned through it all, but He didn't inflict this torture on my daughter so I could learn them. I learned them because I chose to let go of what wasn't mine and hold on, experiencing God's peace and joy that was always there for the taking.

Melissa has wanted to have a baby since the moment she got married. Month after month, year after year, she experienced disappointment. Then, one incredible day, she had great news to share with us. We were all so very excited only to have it fall apart a few short months later. How heart-breaking for her, and heart-breaking for us to watch.

The day after she lost her little one, she came to visit me. She sat on my bed and told me all about her experience at the hospital and how her husband had really stepped up to the plate and been there for her throughout it all. She began to tell me all the really funny things he had done because he'd had little sleep leading up to them going to the hospital. The two of us had a good belly laugh.

She turned to me with tears in her eyes and said, "Where was God in this, Mom?"

All I could think to say was "Melissa, he's here right now with us, bringing us laughter in what is a very sad situation."

Trying to find a reason for the sad and disappointing things that happen in life can be so crippling and life-stopping.

To console those who mourn in Zion, to give them beauty for ashes, the oil of joy for mourning, the garment of praise for the spirit of heaviness; that they may be called trees of righteousness, the planting of the Lord, that He may be glorified.

—Isaiah 61:3, NKJV

Thank goodness this world isn't our home. I think there's enough good down here to make it all worth the journey, but enough suffering to keep us longing for our true home.

chapter twenty-four

PERFECT ISN'T POSSIBLE NOR REQUIRED

THE GUILT IS THE HARDEST HURDLE TO GET OVER FOR THE MOTHER OF AN addict. I spent hours, days, weeks typing out all the texts my daughter and I wrote each other. I don't know if it was a blessing or a curse that I had a cell phone that doesn't delete its text history. I was desperately searching for what I had said during that time to trigger her back into her addiction.

I found phrases like "I love you," "you are doing great," and "it's not how many times you fall, it's how often you get back up." I could find nothing that would warrant the anger and hatred I felt coming from her. The blame was so hurtful. I had to see a counsellor, who said to me, "If your daughter was famous and was getting huge rewards, would you be standing behind her, saying, 'It's all me, I did this,' taking all the credit for her achievements? Why then are you taking all the credit for her failures?"

These words changed my way of thinking.

I began to see that first of all I have two daughters, and each turned out very differently. I also began to look back on the kind of mom I was and what we did together as a family. We had huge struggles, for sure, and went through some very difficult times. I concluded that I was a great mom with some huge challenges, and I did the very best I could. I wasn't a perfect mom, because perfect moms don't exist anywhere, but I realized I was a long way from being a bad mom. Addiction, as I have found, exists in all types of families. There is no set pattern.

chapter twenty-five

HAPPY WITHOUT A HAPPY ENDING

Years ago, I sat in the audience of a women's conference. I was enjoying the speaker, but one thought went through my mind. I was kind of angry at God. I said, "God, why do they always have speakers who have a happy ending? I want to hear from someone who doesn't have that happy ending, to find out how to get through the life I'm living."

Years later, after Ashley called me "evil," I went on a very long walk to my parents' home to escape what was going on at mine. As I walked, tears rolled down my face. I recalled that recently I had shared with a few friends that I thought I was ready to tell my story. At that time, things were going relatively well. It seemed as though the worst was behind us. I started having a conversation with God on that walk to my parents and said, "I won't share my story. I'll keep quiet, if this is what the cost will be." I then recalled the moment long ago where I'd sat in that women's conference longing for a story without a happy ending. Maybe that was the story God wanted me to tell.

Addiction is a lifelong battle, and I don't know when this story will be over. The light at the end of the tunnel is so often another train. There's no better way to describe it. However, in the middle of it I have learned to be happy without a happy ending, and that's the story I tell.

The reality is that very few of our loved ones will make it through addiction without huge costs. Some of them won't survive, and some of us won't survive to see them come through. I went to the darkest place in my mind and said, "Even if she cries out to God in her final breath, I'll take that victory."

I decided to give myself a motto to follow:

What I cannot CONTROL will NOT CONTROL me

I have posted this on my wall, and it is my cell phone screensaver. When something happens, I ask myself, *Can I do anything to change or control this?* If the answer is no, I give it to God and go on. I won't allow it to change me anymore, to make me bitter, to make me powerless. I keep going. It gets easier the more I do it. Letting go becomes the norm instead of being engulfed by what I can do nothing about.

chapter twenty-six

HE ISN'T OURS

MELISSA IS FAMOUS FOR HER VERBAL FAUX PAUS. SHE'S GREAT FOR saying something at the best time that turns a bad situation into something funny. We call them blonde moments, though she's not blonde. She's someone very special who has yet to fully realize her worth.

My personal favourite slip of the tongue happened on my fortieth birthday. The day a woman turns forty isn't usually a day she likes to remember—or at least remember with any significant amount of joy—but thanks to Melissa, I'll always remember my fortieth birthday with a smile and a chuckle.

It was an especially busy day, because it was also exam day for Melissa. At the time, we commuted back and forth to Ancaster from Brantford. Melissa was attending Hamilton District Christian High School and I worked just down the street from the school. Rather than making her sit around all day for me to finish work, I offered to drive her home during my lunch break and told her to call me when she was finished her exam. I would pick her up.

On the way home, she looked at me and with all the sincerity and warmth she could muster and said, "Mom, I just want to thank you for being my mom for the last forty years."

I immediately laughed. "Melissa, I haven't been your mom for forty years"

She laughed, realizing her mistake. After a short pause, she said, "How long have you been my mom anyway?"

I laughed again. "Melissa, how old are you?"

The really frightening thing about this was that the exam she had completed that morning was math.

Then there are times when Melissa will say the most profound things that stop me in my tracks and take hold of my heart. One line she said to me helped me deal with the pain of my beloved grandson being in the middle of all this mess and feeling so powerless to truly protect him.

On the very sad day when we had to return our grandson into the arms of the unknown, Melissa stopped me in my tracks. I was sharing my heart with her when she said, "Mom, he's not ours. He isn't even theirs. He belongs to God."

Grandkids are the most precious gift. Whether they come to us the way we planned or if they are a surprise delight in the middle of disaster, they are precious. I didn't even have dreams of being a grandma, and neither of my daughters expressed a big desire to have kids of their own, so it wasn't something I gave much thought to until the day my grandson was born and I held him in my arms. I knew he was a boy, but I looked down into the face of my daughter whom I'd given birth to so many years ago. It was her face on the child I held, and it was love at first sight. I loved him simply because he was hers. I'd never had a boy, so I wasn't quite sure what to expect, but I quickly learned that boys seem a lot less complicated than what I had experienced having girls.

I've spoken to many grandmas who are in the same situation as me. Their heartbreak is mixed in with the greatest joys of their lives, and that's their precious grandchildren who are right smack dab in the middle of the chaos. Most of the grandparents I speak to are indeed raising these little ones in the prime of their life when they should be enjoying a much slower pace and the rewards of a life of hard work. Instead they're chasing after toddlers, changing diapers, and working extra jobs to pay for it all in their retirement. Our grandson lived with us on a couple of short occasions, and giving him back was heart-stopping. He was hard work, yes, and I really don't know how we managed, but we would do it all over again if the need were there. We hope and pray we'll get to continue to enjoy the gift of being grandparents.

It helps me to think about all the books and testimonies I've heard over the years of kids who were raised in horrible situations. I think of Jim Daly, whose book I read two summers ago. He's now the head of Focus on the Family. I think of Maury Blair and his book and testimony, *The Child of Woe*. Then I remembered the words I texted Ashley, who at one point was worried about her son and how his life would be because of the home she was raising him in. I texted her, "It isn't about a perfect home, a perfect mother or father, it is about a perfect God."

My grandson and I watched a movie together one day. It was called *Kung Fu Panda*. A wise character in the movie made this statement: "Yesterday is history, tomorrow is a mystery, today is a gift." Who knew I could be inspired by a kid's movie? And yet I was. I've learned to really enjoy the good moments like these. They are gifts and are to be treasured, and too often taken for granted. That was a good day.

chapter twenty-seven

JUDGE NOT

I DON'T KNOW ABOUT YOU, BUT MY HUSBAND AND I SIT IN THE SAME seats every Sunday: second row from the front, right side of the church. We're surrounded by the same people every Sunday. One particular Sunday, a young man sat beside us who didn't usually sit there. He was fidgety, loud, and rather annoying. Partway through the service, my husband leaned forward and I knew what was coming. I gave him a look that said "Don't you dare." He immediately understood what I was thinking.

Even though I have often been completely fed up with Ashely—I've been angry, and yes, sometimes even ashamed at her behaviour—I feel as though I'm not qualified to judge her. I haven't walked a day in her shoes. I didn't grow up in a broken home. I haven't suffered from debilitating anxiety issues. I'll never know if I would make the same choices she has. I've never been drunk or high and don't know the hold it can have on one's life.

For those of us who don't know what it's like to suffer with addiction, and can't identify with all the shame and sense of failure one who does feels, we'll never know the kind of courage it takes to walk into a church and sit in a pew amongst us. I knew my husband that day was going to give that young man *the look*. You know that look, the look my friends and I used to get as children when we giggled too much in church or talked too much.

I stopped him because I knew that we didn't know where this young man had come from or what his story was. We needed to just be welcoming and tolerant and thankful that he sat there beside us. He could be my daughter and he could be your son.

When that person shows up in church one day and shares a pew with you, and they aren't dressed appropriately or they smell of cigarettes or alcohol and they don't know how to behave, please make them feel welcome. In all likelihood, they just took the biggest step of their life.

Judge not, that you be not judged. For with what judgment you judge, you will be judged; and with the measure you use, it will be measured back to you. And why do you look at the speck in your brother's eye, but do not consider the plank in your own eye? Or how can you say to your brother, "Let me remove the speck from your eye"; and look, a plank is in your own eye? Hypocrite! First remove the plank from your own eye, and then you will see clearly to remove the speck from your brother's eye. Do not give what is holy to the dogs; nor cast your pearls before swine, lest they trample them under their feet, and turn and tear you in pieces.

Ask, and it will be given to you; seek, and you will find; knock, and it will be opened to you. For everyone who asks receives, and he who seeks finds, and to him who knocks it will be opened. Or what man is there among you who, if his son asks for bread, will give him a stone? Or if he asks for a fish, will he give him a serpent? If you then, being evil, know how to give good gifts to your children, how much more will your Father who is in heaven give good things to those who ask Him!

Therefore, whatever you want men to do to you, do also to them, for this is the Law and the Prophets.

—Matthew 7:1–12, NKJV

WHERE THINGS ARE

AT THE TIME I'M WRITING THIS, MY DAUGHTER HAS BEEN CLEAN AND sober for over six months. She has an amazing job with full benefits and continues to engage in her counselling. We still get regular visits from our grandson, who starts school this fall. He continues to be an absolute delight to us. Things seem to be going very well for their little family. They seem to be on the right track, and motivated to stay that way. The past dictates how hopeful we feel. We're realistic, but we continue to pray for success each and every day.

I'm still on the outside of her life and I continue to take comfort in the story of Joseph and the time it took for healing to take place in that family. We have forgiven, but our trust has been fractured. I know that one day healing will begin. We'll all be ready when that day comes, because God's timing is perfect.

Just yesterday, Ron and I sat on the couch with our grandson between us. He cuddled close to us. We looked at each other and agreed that life doesn't get much better than this. We were truly thankful.

Life didn't go as planned for me or my children, but we aren't finished. I don't know what the future holds for Ashley, but I do know that I'll be okay. It won't be easy, but I know I'll get through it because

I know in my knower, and deep down in my soul, that my God will get me through.

Let's be real for a moment. I'm human. I still get angry at injustices. I still cry when I think about Ashley. I miss her and think of fond memories, and there are many of those. I'm still concerned for their future, but I'm no longer slave to those feelings. I can process them more quickly and move on. I no longer climb into the pit and stay there until life gets better. Life may never get better, so why waste time waiting? I put one foot in front of the other and do what I can, and let God do what I can't.

Shortly after Ashley finished rehab, CAS called a meeting for all those involved in my grandson's case. This would be the first time I'd see her in months, and I suspected it would be difficult for me. The meeting went on for hours and I could feel the hatred coming from my daughter across the table. I was screaming inside, barely able to endure what I couldn't understand. Didn't she know how much I love her? Didn't she know how much this was killing me, how much I'd given up for her and done for her? Didn't she realize that every difficult decision I'd made was to save her life? When the meeting finally came to a close, I couldn't wait to escape. My eyes were on the back entrance and I made a beeline for it as soon as I was able. I waited outside and welcomed the cold air.

When Ron and I finally got into the car and made our way home, the floodgates opened wide. I wailed and cried with sobs that came from deep within my soul. My whole body shook. I could tell my husband was terrified, so between sobs I got out the words, "It's okay. I'm going to be okay. I just need to get this out."

When we arrived home, Melissa was there waiting for us. Though I was a mess on the outside, I reassured her, too, that I would be okay. Ron dismissed himself and said he would be right back. When he returned, he held in his arms the biggest bag of potato chips. We laughed.

I had developed some addictions of my own over the past couple of years. Though my high cholesterol tells me I should avoid them, I took great comfort in family-size bags of potato chips. I also mastered an even greater addiction to Candy Crush, and presently I'm in the middle of Level 450. This is an accomplishment.

I ate the bag of chips, and by Sunday I was into the full-blown anger stage of grief. I proceeded to reorganize the house. I might as well put the anger to good use, and it did feel good. By Monday morning, I was okay again. I understood that being human, I would grieve, but having let go the way I had so many months ago, I knew I would get through it. I've mastered getting through the stages of grief at lightning speed.

The next CAS meeting was held a month later, and I was fine. That evening, I even went out to a women's conference and thoroughly enjoyed it. Life goes on.

Tonight Ron and I were invited to the home Ashley shares with her partner and son. She wouldn't be there; while she was at work, her partner had invited us over. Our grandson had just had minor surgery and was a very brave boy. I wanted so badly to go and give him his favourite treat of cheesy Dorito's.

After giving some thought to whether I was ready to face his father, I decided I would go. My husband and I were warmly welcomed and conversation flowed easily. I know it must have been just as hard for him as it was for me. I'm that mother-in-law he cannot please. I've given him a piece of my mind on more than one occasion, and rightfully so at times, but still I'm sure he doesn't see me as his favourite person in the world. I was proud of us both when I walked away. Very proud.

On the way home, Ron held my hand and said to me, "I'm so proud of you."

"I'm proud of me, too, and I'm proud of him." I felt God giving me a miracle, because I had faced something I thought I never could.

When I got home, my phone was ringing. Melissa was on the line. When I told her what I had just done, she couldn't believe it. She told me she had just been praying for me. It's so cool to know how God is working behind the scenes. Sometimes we see it, and sometimes we just have to trust Him in the silence and be patient.

Many years ago, I wrote this poem while thinking about what we go through when we grieve, or any difficult situation, and how we get so focussed on what we've lost that we lose sight of what we still have. More importantly, we lose sight of where all good gifts come from.

THE GIFT GIVER

The gift I'd received
I couldn't believe
This precious gift
Could be for me

I loved and cared for it
Treasured and embraced it

My life was full
Content and complete
All of life's blessings
Sat right at my feet

Then one day the gift was gone
It took a part of me

I couldn't believe
This gift of mine
Would now only be
Just a moment in time

The laughter faded, the pain so great
Could it be that this was my fate?

Remembering my gift
My gift, my treasure
A gift so grand
No cup could measure

My life now so torn and withered
My eyes were on the gift, not on the Giver

It would be a year and half before I heard the words "I love you, mom" via text. With those words she entered back into a relationship with me. I am not ashamed of what she has been through. It isn't who she is. I am proud of what she is overcoming. I have no guarantee that when life happens she won't reach for the drugs again but I know that she has everything in her life to be successful. The choice is hers. My choice is to allow God to be my compass, my comforter and my strength. I do not know what my future holds but I know who holds my future.

I leave you with what has become one of my favourite verses in the Bible:

Be still, and know that I am God; I will be exalted among the nations, I will be exalted in the earth!

—Psalm 46:10, NKJV

THE TITLE

One of my closest friends and I used to laugh and say that one day we were going to write a book and call it *When the Light at the End of the Tunnel Is Another Train.* It fits both of our lives for very different reasons. Now that I look back, I think there are two lights at the end of that tunnel. One is the oncoming train, whatever that might be. It's coming and there's no stopping it, but there's a light that shines brighter than that of the train. That light is my heavenly father, who's right there lighting the way, steering my path. We can choose to follow the light of the train or the light of our Saviour.

If you knew me outside of this story, you'd know that I have an awesome though at times twisted sense of humour. I hope you see the humour in my title, even though the subject matter isn't funny. One of my favourite things about my family is our laughter. No amount of pain has ever taken that away. For a time, yes, but it's never permanent.

HELPFUL RESOURCES

A Family Support Group

Max Lucado, *You'll Get Through This: Hope and Help for Your Turbulent Times* (Nashville, TN: Thomas Nelson, 2013).

Carol Kent, *When I Lay My Isaac Down: Unshakable Faith in Unthinkable Circumstances* (Carol Stream, IL: NavPress, 2014)

Elisa Morgan, *The Beauty of Broken: My Story and Likely Yours Too* (Carol Stream, IL: NavPress, 2013)

Jim Daly and Bob DeMoss, *Finding Home* (Colorado Springs, CO: David C. Cook, 2011)

ABOUT THE AUTHOR

Judy is the youngest daughter of Rev. Lorne Shepherd, founder of Heart to Heart Family Ministries. She gave her heart to Christ at a young age and suffered very few real life struggles until she reached her adult years. Life then was a series of heart-breaking experiences, from being the victim of adultery and divorce to being a single parent. Nothing challenged her faith more than her daughter's battle with addictions.

As a form of therapy, she has written her way through this journey and has chosen to share this in hopes that it may help the countless Christian moms out there who are suffering in silence.

In Judy's teen years and early twenties, she appeared on Christian television shows *100 Huntley Street* and *Just for Us*. She worked for several years at Crossroads Christian Communications Inc. in the Professional Counselling Department as their front desk assistant, where she also led a support group for single mothers.

Judy presently serves on an advisory council for St. Leonard's Community Centre in Brantford, Ontario, a centre that assists families and individuals who suffer with addictions and/or mental health issues. She also works part-time for the Ontario Alliance of Christian Schools.

Judy and her husband Ron are members of Evangel Pentecostal Church in Brantford. She has recently started a group called Christian Mothers of Addicts, which meets once a month. This is a cause near and dear to her heart, because the emotional and spiritual load a mother carries when dealing with this issue is too much to bear alone.

Judy is available for speaking engagements.
Please contact her at time2catchup@hotmail.com

CPSIA information can be obtained
at www.ICGtesting.com
Printed in the USA
BVHW071244300120
570970BV00006B/719